SYNERGY
A Collage of Voices

*Maryland Writers' Association
Anthology 2014*

SYNERGY
A Collage of Voices

Maryland Writers' Association
Anthology 2014

Apprentice House
Loyola University Maryland
Baltimore, Maryland

First Edition

Printed in the United States of America

Paperback ISBN: 978-1-62720-089-9
E-book ISBN: 978-1-62720-090-5

Design by Apprentice House

Published by Apprentice House

Apprentice House
Loyola University Maryland
4501 N. Charles Street
Baltimore, MD 21210
410.617.5265 • 410.617.2198 (fax)
www.ApprenticeHouse.com
info@ApprenticeHouse.com

MARYLAND
WRITERS'
ASSOCIATION

The Maryland Writers' Association (MWA) is a voluntary, not-for-profit organization dedicated to supporting the art, business, and craft of writing in all its forms. The MWA strives to:

- Bring together aspiring, emerging, and established writers of all genres and disciplines,
- Serve as an information and networking resource,
- Help members make contacts that lead to publication,
- Encourage writers to reach their full potential, and,
- Promote writing within Maryland communities.

In keeping with the MWA's mission, a national poetry and prose (fiction and creative nonfiction) contest was held in 2014. This anthology is a compilation of the winners' work in each genre.

We are grateful to all the judges who participated in evaluating the submissions:
Lalita Noronha, MWA President / www.lalitanoronha.com
Holly Morse-Ellington, MWA Vice President / www.hollyneat.com

Dominique Cahn
Emily Rich
Lynn Stansbury
Pat Valdata

A special thanks to the judges of our finalists:
Ned Balbo (Poetry)
Susan Muaddi Darraj (Fiction and Creative Nonfiction)

We'd also like to thank Apprentice House Press for this partnership with the MWA. The MWA couldn't achieve its goals for its members without such a supportive community of writers, editors, and publishers.

CONTENTS

JASON'S CAP

Barbara Mujica

He seemed pretty much like all the other soldiers to whom I'd rented rooms. Square jaw. Broad shoulders. Reserved demeanor. He was leaving the military, he said. He'd done four tours in Iraq and two in Afghanistan, and he'd served on bases in Texas and Virginia. Now it was time to move on. For the time being he had a job at a bakery, where he was using one of the skills he'd learned in the Army: baking bread. But he was going to study electrical engineering at the local community college. There was nothing wrong with being a baker, he assured me, but he wanted more out of life than that. I liked him. I didn't hesitate for a moment before assigning him the room that had belonged to my eldest daughter, Adriana. She was married now and out of the house. I handed him the keys.

"This one opens the front door, and this one is for your bedroom. Your rent is due the first of the month."

"Okay," he said.

He had a quiet, detached way about him. He picked up his duffle bag and headed upstairs.

"There are a few rules at Mrs. Montez's place," I said matter-of-factly when he came down to sign the contract. "Not many, but a few."

"Yeah?" I thought there was a slight smugness to his tone, but I didn't attach any importance to it. The young veterans who rented my rooms had been subjected to so many *rules* for such a long time that they flinched at the word. Still, when you're a single woman living in a house with a bunch of men, you have to set some limits.

"No smoking in the rooms. No guns or other weapons. No porn in visible places. You can use the kitchen at any time, but aside from coffee, you'll have to supply your own food unless you want to eat dinner here. If you do, let me know the day before. I serve at seven sharp. Be prompt and appropriately dressed. No bare feet. No baseball caps. No rough language at the table. We all treat each other with respect. I think that's it."

He listened without comment. I handed him the contract and watched him sign it: Jason Albemarle. He had a robust signature, with full, clear letters that listed slightly to the right, like hardy sailors steadying themselves against the tilt of the stern. I signed my name by the word "Proprietor": Jacqueline Montez.

"Okay, Jacky," he said, throwing the document and the pen on the table. "See you tonight."

I raised my eyebrows. "I know I'm a bit old-fashioned," I said calmly, "but I prefer to be called Mrs. Montez. At any rate, I never use the nickname 'Jacky.'" He gawked at me, eyes bulging like hard-boiled eggs. I felt as though I'd asked him to wear a tutu to dinner. "The other young men all call me Mrs. Montez," I said dryly. "Of course, I will be glad to address you any way you want."

"Just call me Jason," he replied. His jaw dropped slightly, becoming all gristly and stiff.

I didn't care. A widow living alone in a house with six or eight young men has to keep her distance. You have to make it clear that you're not their pal. You can help them out when they need it—write a character reference for a job, for example, or recommend a dentist—but you have to make it clear that you are the landlady, not their friend, and that on the first of the month, you expect to collect the rent. No exceptions. No leniency. Anyhow, I was old enough to be the mother of any of them. My son Ignacio, who had come back from Iraq in the spring and was now living in Chicago, was in his thirties already. Jason could damn well call me Mrs. Montez.

The following Sunday he came down for breakfast just as I was getting home from Mass.

"Good morning, *Mrs. Montez*," he sniggered.

I usually didn't see him in the mornings. He had to be at the bakery at four in the morning, long before I'd left for my job at the bank.

"How are you, *Mrs. Montez?*" He had a pinched-faced grin, as though he carried a wad of bitters under his tongue.

I thought: Sorry it bothers you, son, but just suck it up. I didn't say it out loud, though. He was wearing a backward baseball cap, and I had the impression it was meant as a provocation. I overlooked it. I really didn't care what he wore except in my dining room at dinnertime.

I handed him the newspaper. "Want it?"

He took it from me, glanced at the headlines, and threw it back on the table.

"There's coffee in the pot," I added.

Corey Frater came into the kitchen and sat down at the table. "Morning, Mrs. M," he said jovially. Of all the young men to whom I'd rented rooms after Ignacio deployed, Corey was my favorite. I'd started taking in boarders for the money, of course, but also for the company. I liked having young military men around. They reminded me of my son and eased the anxiety. After all, they had returned from the war, hadn't they? Ignacio would return too, I kept telling myself. I'd given Corey the sewing room. He was a polite, soft-spoken young man, a Marine staff sergeant who had done recon in Iraq. He was from somewhere in the South—Georgia, I think—and his manners were from another epoch. If he ever said *damn* or even *jerk*, he excused himself first. For example, he'd say, "The guy's a...excuse me for saying this, ma'am...but the guy's a jerk."

"I'm gonna get some coffee," he announced, getting up. "Can I get you something, ma'am?"

"You're *supposed* to call her *Mrs. Montez*," snapped Jason.

Corey stared at him as though he had a penis growing out of his forehead. Jason hesitated a moment, then turned and sauntered out the back door.

"We have to be patient with him," I said after an uneasy pause. "Maybe he's suffering from PTSD."

"Maybe he's just a…excuse me, ma'am…Maybe he's just a moron."

"Who knows what he went through over there, what he saw. Don't be harsh, Corey. Some of these young men suffered so much…"

"Pardon me for disagreeing," countered Corey. "We all saw a lot of bad stuff over there. There's no excuse for that kind of behavior. Listen, Mrs. M, if you make an omelet and it doesn't come out, what does that mean?"

"I guess it means you made a mistake."

"You can't make a mistake whipping up an omelet. If you make a bad omelet, it means you started out with bad eggs. Some of these guys were already nut cases when they went into the military."

"I think Jason's just immature. We have to be compassionate."

"Bah! He should have grown up by now. Anyhow, he didn't live through any horror stories in the Middle East."

"How do you know?"

"He was never in combat."

"He told me he served in Iraq and Afghanistan!"

"In his dreams! He was in Kuwait three times. That's all."

"But why would he lie?"

"Some of these guys who weren't in the thick of it…they're embarrassed, they make up stories. But I know for sure that he was never there."

I must have looked flabbergasted because Corey laughed and said, "Recon, remember? I was in reconnaissance."

A couple of weeks later, Jason cornered me in the morning and told me he was planning to be home that evening for dinner. I didn't think to ask why he wasn't at the bakery already, but I don't remember that he looked as though anything were wrong. He'd never had dinner with us before because he usually got home from work in the late afternoon and went right to bed. Baker's hours—4 a.m. to 4 p.m.

"Okay, that's fine," I said. He was supposed to have let me know the day before, but I let it go. The stew was already bubbling in the crockpot, and the kitchen was redolent with Moroccan spices, lamb, and garlic. I always made extra, so I knew there'd be enough. "See you tonight," I called as I ran out the door.

The air was leaden. A storm was brooding on the horizon like an angry giant. By noon the monster had begun to heave clouds like murky, wet, tattered blankets over the sky. Restless gusts battered roofs. The heavens growled. By early afternoon drops like pitchforks were stabbing the lantana in the flower bed in front of the house. The trees shivered and begged for mercy.

Jason blew through the door about a half hour after the rest of us had begun eating.

"You were supposed to be here at seven," snapped Dan Lesko, a no-nonsense Marine as punctual as a German.

"Fuck you!" snarled Jason.

We all turned to stare at him. Corey shook his head in disgust.

"It's raining, in case you hadn't noticed, assholes! It's not so easy to get around on the buses."

"He means, 'Excuse me, ma'am. Sorry I'm late,'" said Corey, turning toward me. His distaste for Jason was palpable.

"I don't need you to tell her what I mean, asshole," snapped Jason. "I can speak! I have a mouth." He slouched down in his chair and ate his Moroccan stew without saying another word.

"It's delicious," said Dan. "A terrific stew, Mrs. M."

"Absolutely terrific," Corey agreed.

After that I noticed that Jason no longer left the house in the dead of night to get to the bakery at 4 a.m. or went to bed in the afternoon. However, he rarely joined us for dinner.

"Did you get another job?" I asked him one Sunday afternoon. I was mending some towels in the kitchen.

"You got your check on time this month, didn't you?"

"Yes, Jason," I said serenely. "I did."

His forehead was pale and lackluster under the visor of his baseball cap, but his eyes were feverish. He had the look of an impassioned martyr bracing for the arrows that would inevitably pierce his body. His gaze was steady. Defiant. The arrows would come but he wouldn't wince.

"Something is the matter with that boy," I kept telling myself. "He has been through some trauma." But I didn't know exactly what it was or what to do about it.

It occurred to me that I should check his room. As a rule I never entered my boarders' quarters. Each man was responsible for his own space and had his own key. I had a master, of course, but I didn't snoop. The men had use of the laundry room and washed their own clothes, changed their own sheets, and cleaned their own floors. I had no reason to invade anyone's privacy. And yet I was worried about Jason. What if he was on drugs? What if he had some serious medical condition? Or had lost his job? I knew nothing about his family. I couldn't get in touch with his mother. Did he even have a mother?

The next morning I asked for an hour's leave at the bank and returned home at about 11:00. The house appeared to be empty. I tiptoed around and knocked at all the doors. I was especially cautious when I got to Jason's. I couldn't risk his catching me in the room. He might fly off the handle and do something rash.

I slipped the key into the lock. Adriana had loved lavender as a little girl, and my husband, Alejandro, and I had given in to her passion. Lavender walls with purple trim, lavender and pink flowered curtains, a lavender teddy bear, and an American Girl doll in a lavender nightgown. All that was gone now, of course. I had painted the room beige and brown when I started taking in boarders. Plain white venetian blinds. A utilitarian desk and chairs, with a sturdy dresser and bed.

Jason hadn't done much decorating. The walls were bare. No family photographs. In fact, no photographs at all. No computer. No books. No knickknacks. No military medals. I looked around for clues—a pill bottle, for example, or an alarming doodle on a notepad. Nothing.

I peeked into his closet. It was almost empty. A couple of pants thrown over hangers, two button-down shirts, a lone belt hanging on a belt rack.

I was loath to pull open his drawers, but I did. The first held a couple of crumpled T-shirts and a wad of money. Also a Swiss army knife with an exposed blade. The next one was empty except for one menacing object—a hard, black body like that of an overgrown cockroach or a horseshoe crab. It was a Glock 19. I knew because Alejandro had always kept a gun in the house for protection, and he'd had one just like it. After he died, I got rid of it.

I left the room. I wasn't sure what to do. I didn't want Jason to know I'd opened his drawer, but I also didn't want that gun in my house. I had told him the rules.

Back at work I was nervous and distracted. I was afraid I was going to make a mistake with somebody's money. That evening I waited until Corey returned home from the college, where he was taking courses in management, and pulled him aside.

"I can't be sure," I lied, "and don't ask me why I think this, but I suspect one of the men has a gun in his room."

Corey's answer took me aback. "It wouldn't surprise me," he said. "It's part of the culture. I'm sure every guy here owns a weapon."

I was speechless.

"Even me. But mine's out of reach, inaccessible. Anyway, don't worry about it. We all know the power of a firearm, and we're all trained in how to use one responsibly."

"But I *am* worried," I whispered. Did this mean that all of my boarders were flaunting the rules? I decided this wasn't the time to ask.

"You're concerned about Jason, right? I'll take care of it," Corey said coolly.

"You can't use your recon skills to sneak into his room and steal his gun."

"I'll have a talk with him," Corey said. "Tomorrow I have an early class, but on Friday I'll catch him before I go to school. He usually has breakfast at a little café by the college. He lost his job at the bakery, so he probably reads want ads on his iPhone and then goes out on interviews. I'm pretty sure he'll hand over his gun without an argument."

I felt better after that.

The next day I was just pulling out of the driveway when I noticed Jason sitting on the steps in front of the house. I waved to him through the car window.

"Hey, Mrs. Montez," he called after me. I braked. He approached the car with his hands in his pockets, and even though I wasn't really afraid, I shuddered. "Listen, I'll be here for dinner tonight, okay?"

"Sure," I said, "fine. But in the future, please let me know the day before. We have rules, remember?" I tried to make myself sound as innocuous as possible.

Things went smoothly at the bank that morning, but in the afternoon there was a mix-up about a funds transfer from Abu Dhabi, which I finally had to get the central office to straighten out. I was bushed by the time I got home and was glad I'd left the coq-au-vin in the crock pot in the morning.

Jason came into the dining room wearing an Orioles baseball cap and a torn T-shirt. He looked as though he'd just pulled himself out of bed. He sprawled onto the chair and sat hunched and wide-legged, staring at his rolls and butter as though they were very important. For a while no one said anything.

"Jason," I ventured finally, "I would appreciate it if you would please remove your cap. I'm a bit old-fashioned, I know, but I'd consider it a special favor."

He straightened up and removed his cap. Another awkward silence.

"Great chicken, Mrs. M," Dan said finally.

"Yes, it is," added Corey.

The others echoed the compliment, and before long the incident had been forgotten. The subject had turned to the job market. There were openings in security and defense, if you wanted to go that route, someone was saying, but there was no real money in it. Better to go back to school and get a degree in business, said someone else. Morgan Stanley had jobs and so did Booz Allen. Was it better to pay a professional outfit to do your resume or just do it yourself, Dan Lesko wanted to know. A while later the conversation meandered over to football.

After dinner was over, I gathered up the dishes, then stuffed the garbage into a plastic bag to take out to the pail.

It was a clear, frosty night. With my free hand I pulled my collar up around my ears. Leaves crackled underfoot. The low growl of the wind—something like the ron-ron of an anxious cat—muffled my footsteps. For an instant I thought I heard, or sensed, someone following me, but I looked around and saw only the opalescent pallor of the moon. I moved forward in the darkness toward the shed where I kept the trash. I could discern the silhouette in the moonlight. Suddenly I heard someone call. I turned. It was Jason.

"Mrs. Montez, I'd like to have a word with you."

"Of course, Jason."

I thought it was strange that he'd followed me outside to talk but I wasn't frightened. I couldn't imagine that he would do something terrible right there in the yard.

"I want to tell you something." He was standing about two feet from me, and now I could see clearly that he was seething. He'd been nursing a low-grade rage for a while. But why? I'd tried to be fair, to overlook small irritations, and treat him with the same respect as everyone else.

"Listen, *Jacky*," he said with the same mocking tone I'd heard before, "you have no fucking business telling me what to wear. What I do and what I wear is...none...of...your...goddamn...fucking...business." He enunciated every syllable, spitting it out and into my face.

I had to bite my lip to keep from laughing. All this rage over a baseball cap?

"I'm not telling you what to wear, Jason," I said as sweetly as I could. "However, as I'm sure you know, it's considered disrespectful for a gentleman to wear a hat indoors in mixed company. Some people don't take those old rules very seriously anymore, but since you're going out into the professional world, and you never know what other people's sensitivities may be, it's a good idea to respect these social niceties to stay on the safe side. After all, why put yourself at a disadvantage? That's why I insist on the traditional rules of courtesy at dinnertime. Nothing personal."

Anyway, I thought, it's my house and I make the rules. But of course I didn't say it.

He stood there, his eyes waxy in the moonlight. His whole being oozed loathing.

I turned and headed toward the shed. When I emerged, he was gone.

I was afraid I wouldn't be able to sleep that night, so I took a couple of Advil PMs and went to bed.

When I came down the next morning, Corey, Dan, and two or three others were huddled in the kitchen, murmuring.

"Did anyone get the newspaper?" I asked, suddenly nervous.

"Don't go out there, ma'am," said Corey softly.

I looked from one to the other.

"It's Jason. We found him sprawled out on the lawn this morning, head blown to pieces, blood everywhere. He used his Glock."

"His baseball cap flew clear into the bushes," added Dan. "It's shredded."

I crumpled onto a chair. "We already called the police," said Corey.

"But I didn't mean to criticize him," I stammered. "I wasn't telling him what to wear. It's just that…"

"It's nothing you did, ma'am," said Corey, laying his strong, consoling hand on my shoulder. "The guy had a lot of problems."

I was sobbing disconsolately. "I didn't mean to hurt him," I kept repeating.

"Like I once told you, ma'am," said Corey, "when you get a lousy omelet, it's usually because you started with a lousy egg."

I shook my head. I felt as though I had a mouth full of dirt.

Bush Taxi

Debra McGhee

"This really happened," you imagine writing as you catch your last sight of the bush taxi—the first one—through the back window of the new bus, which will finally carry you to Birnin Konni. "I don't want you think that I'm playing with reality, pushing the facts around to make a tidy metaphor. The bush taxi engine—that first bush taxi—caught fire between Bouza and Konni."

You'll write it all down in a letter and send it off. This is your diary method—letter-writing. Friends back home have urged you to keep a journal of your time teaching in West Africa but you rebel. Instead, your memories will be carried by the wind and scattered across miles.

In Africa women separate millet from chaff like this: They pound the whole grain in a knee-high wooden mortar, then carry the broken pieces in broad, sand-colored calabashes on their heads out into the fields. They stand with the wind blowing across them. They place an empty calabash on the ground. The full calabash they hold high above their heads and slowly tilt. The grain pours out. The wind catches the empty, fluffy chaff and lifts it away. The heavy kernels fall straight down and the lower calabash slowly fills with grain to satisfy the day's hunger. The sturdy dark arms shining against the sky, the snowy drifts of chaff accumulating at the side of each woman, and the blind and perfect sorting of wind and weight all greatly please you.

And so you write letters.

This really happened.

You made Madaou by 4:00 p.m. Even at that hour, on the perimeter of evening, the sky was a blank white sheet and the wind rolling off the pavement and through the broken window of the dented van—the bush taxi— was so hot it seemed the world was burning. T.S. Eliot must have known West Africa, you think, to write "April is the cruelest month."

An old woman sits beside you wearing a transparent blue veil over her head. Although your hip is squeezed against hers by the bulky man on your right, although you can't move your arm without brushing the spongy softness of her breast, the old woman stares fixedly ahead, the skin of her face caught and pulled into tight slanting wrinkles by the narrow arch of her nose. As the wind blasts the bush taxi, the woman's veil lifts and trails silkily over your forearms. You remark upon the simple elegance of the cloth. You look down at your own wilted cotton dress, at the sweat stain spreading between your breasts, and the prickly heat splotching your pale arms. It has been a long time since you felt appropriate.

At the first police stop after Madaou you are made to wait 40 minutes while the gendarmes, their machine guns propped carelessly against a wooden bench, eat balls of rice and sauce with their hands and flirt with two of bush taxi's young female passengers. You note how the girls lean their elbows on a low wooden table and lift their bottoms tight against the purple, gold, and red of their skirts. Their smiles dance like lightening at midnight. Little beads of sweat work their way up through the forests of dark looping braids to sparkle as they laugh and toss their heads. The old male passengers watch and sigh and wander to the side of the road to unroll their woven mats and pray.

Later, 75 kilometers from the gendarmes' station, the bush taxi abruptly veers off the road and stops. You are shaken out of a daydream by the rattling of the van over desert ruts and rubble and by a final cough from the engine that fills the crowded back seats with smoke. The driver turns, throws open a metal door covering a part of the engine that juts into the cab and shouts *"C'est un feu!"* People begin to heave themselves toward the bus doors. The long, full gowns of the old men spread like wings as they jump from the high back ledge of the bus. You hit the ground surrounded by billowing white cotton.

As you cross the road, a Belgian doctor of your acquaintance speeds by in a shiny green station wagon. The windows are rolled up and he looks straight ahead—not into the bush where the startled passengers are coughing and wandering around the smoking bus. Dashing back into the center of the road, you jump and wave your arms. But the station wagon quickly recedes behind the oily waves of heat rising from the blacktop. The desert swallows the roar of its engine.

You pull a roll of cloth out of your backpack and spread it on the ground. You settle yourself with legs tucked under you and off to one side, and close your eyes.

Back home, in Washington, on an April evening like this, you might have walked across the Calvert Street Bridge and watched the sun set behind the gothic turrets and peaked roofs that filigreed the skyline. You would have seen the lights come on in random windows, each misted golden pane insinuating dinner simmering, music summoned up, a quiet conversation, him searching the drawer for a cork screw; her peeling carrots, belly pressed against clean white porcelain. Pausing midway on Calvert Bridge, you might have lost yourself in the lushness of Rock Creek Park, all its ivied excess sprawling beneath the bridge and creeping up its struts, up the hill, up the foundations of apartment buildings, murmuring a dewy chlorophyll promise, "just give me time—I'll grow you all over. I'll wind myself through your mortar and with a thousand tender tendrils pull your wrought iron down. I'll cover your gables with honeysuckle, root into your pipes and power-lines; slowly strangle your little dogs."

The air would be pregnant water. So much water! It glistened in leaves like saucers; penetrated the soft black belly of the earth, fathered promiscuous propagation. Vines and roots, tendrils and trunks, stems and creeping mold, all were haloed by buzzing, intoxicated bees. The shameless musk of pollen would thicken the evening air until a simple inhalation made you accessory to all that copulation. You would be carried along by a rich satisfaction caught under your diaphragm, crowding your heart and lungs.

But not tonight. Tonight you are in Africa and your heart is hardened and still. You have become a camera, working simply to see, knowing that meaning is beyond you here.

Here the miles of coarse sand are littered with black, ragged-edged rocks and scrub brush. In three-sided straw shelters on a rickety wooden table, in town after town, cigarettes, crackers, sugar, tinned milk, and tiny hard candies are sold by the piece. The shopkeepers squat on low stools in a shadowy corner, smoking cigarettes, swatting flies, and shouting at the occasional stray sheep who inches toward the table extending a long black tongue to steal a sugar cube.

At the village wells the women bend double to haul water from the earth. Plump, sticky babies drowse on their backs, dazed by the twin warmth of flesh and sun. The women pull, the babies rock drowsily forward, and the well ropes slide groaning over the thick branch traversing the well, worn shiny smooth as marble by generations of women pulling. A measure of water comes swinging into the light, cradled in a shining rubber sack fashioned from a discarded truck tire inner tube. The rubber tilts and the water dribbles into a waiting, rusted drum, formerly used for petroleum. Then the rubber drops again. Day after day it continues, year after year, this business of getting a drop of water to wash the dust from your throat. The baby on the back is replaced by one younger who grows and eventually takes her turn herself, knotting the fabric sling that binds her own baby to her, high and tight across her breasts, as she reaches for the rope.

On the road between Madaou and Konni the swollen sun now hangs low over the savannah. Along the side of the road the Hausa women spread their cloths—scarlet, royal blue, electric yellow, neon orange—over the ground and scatter themselves like wild flowers. Pushing their blouses up, they nurse their babies and talk and rock as the sun sinks. On the other side of the road, the men empty their plastic canteens and splash their faces. They face east, and begin the day's last prayers. The driver slides a mat under the bus, lays down upon it, and shimmies beneath the vehicle, chin first, to have a look. His helper stands to the side, smoking a cigarette and holding a wrench. Everyone is at peace.

"Excuse me, Miss, do you have a match?"

You look up into a broad smile, a face as wide as pumpkin, with a tidy trimmed mustache that reminds you, weirdly, of Charlie Chaplin. You don't answer but rummage through your bag, retrieving matches and your own cigarettes. Mr. Chaplin lights your cigarette and then his own. "May I?" he asks, with a graceful sweep of his hand toward the dirt.

"Help yourself," you answer.

"You're American, aren't you?"

"Yes."

"It's easy to tell. Only Americans ride these bush taxis—and Nigeriens, of course. Peace Corps, *ne c'est pas?*"

You pull on the cigarette and enjoy the roundness of his voice, the weight of him sitting nearby. You stare down at his feet, at the line where pink flesh meets brown, where the sole ends. Below the line the desert has sucked the skin dry and left it riddled with cracks; above the line, the skin is brown and smooth as a cocoa bean. You look into his face, and at his broad shoulders tilting inward as he leans back on his hands, his cigarette held between his lips at a jaunty angle, the soft fabric of his "bou-bou"—a simple cotton gown—laying over the slight swell of his stomach.

"It's a mess, isn't it?" he says, jerking his head in the direction of the front of the bus. The driver and two other men are now huddled around the engine shining flashlights into it. "You wait and wait only to putter down the road and stop. *Comme ça.* If I were a lizard I would call this home and be done with traveling."

"Where are you headed?" you ask.

"Dosso. I have to bring my wife back. She went there to be with her mother when our child was born."

"*Sannu, sannu,*" you say. It is a Hausa word of greeting and congratulations. You pull your legs up to your chest and squint over the cigarette. "Your first child?"

"Our second. The first died. He became ill after his scarification."

"*Asha,*" you mutter.

"Yes. *Asha.*" Mr. Chaplin puts out his cigarette on the ground and looks away for a moment. Then he turns back to you and asks in a lighter voice "Are you a teacher?"

"Yes. At Lycee Sarrounia Mangou. English, of course. And you?"

"A teacher also. Science. At the CEG in Bouza. I have to laugh to think of myself as a teacher. At least I should understand my students who don't like school. I hated it at first."

"How did you come to go to college then? I mean, you could have been a farmer."

"A farmer!" He spits on the ground by his side, but when he turns to face you the corners of his eyes are creased. "I am Fulani, can't you see?" he touches his breastbone lightly, just above his heart.

"I would rather eat dirt than farm it." He looks away and then continues.

"Twenty years ago, when I was a child, Lake Chad was full. The land was green and it was a paradise to us Fulani. We were all in the bush with our animals all day. Drinking milk all day. Getting fat on mangos. I remember putting my sleeping mat under a full mango tree and just reaching up and 'plop' you see. I could just take a mango whenever I wanted one.

"My father had fourteen wives and 36 children. And we were happy.

"Then one day the government decided we needed to be educated. They just took the children. The parents were heartbroken. The children were locked in the classrooms. If you wanted to go out, you were accompanied by a teacher and another student—not your friend! The children were tied to trees near the school to sleep at night. Like this, *attache*." He threw out his arms and tilted his head back to show how they had slept. "This is true. If they hadn't tied us up there wouldn't have been one student in the morning."

My parents came to see me and said, 'at night, we will wait for you at such and such place in the bush.' I got away and ran, I think, 20 kilometers in the dark. But I couldn't find them. In the morning I was hiding in the trees. The school officials came and found me.

"Later, when the rain stopped and the animals started dying, the Americans like you came." he smiled at her and held a match between his cupped hands, lighting another cigarette.

"Someone offered me a chance to go with them to the United States. But my father said 'No—If you go you won't come back—no more than the rains.

"So the government trained me to be a science teacher. Now I go and sit with my father and say, 'If I had gone, I could be a great doctor today.'"

Darkness settles over the road and the moon is slow in rising. Someone brings out a radio and "Voice of America's" Hausa language broadcast begins. The words "America" "Libya" "Reagan" and "Thatcher" bubble up out of the fast flowing stream of incomprehensible syllables. The white cotton gowns of the men glow dimly when the moon finally lifts herself out of the dirt and drifts heavenward. The men sit on their mats with their arms wrapped around their knees, their bodies still and straight.

The men working on the bus have dragged a tree branch onto the road and started a fire. They have pulled a long metal piece from the engine, are trying to do some blacksmithing on it-heating and pounding the damaged part.

"Listen," you say to Mr. Chaplin. "I have to get home tonight. I have no more water or food, and I have papers to correct. I'm going to try to borrow the driver's flashlight."

"I understand. *Bonne Chance*. Go with Allah."

You approach the driver and briefly explain your needs.

"May I use your flashlight to signal a passing car?"

"But they may be full."

"Still, I have to try."

The men working on the engine stop to watch in amusement as you begin signaling. The first bush taxi is full. The next car, a private one, does not stop. By the time the third car, a nearly empty bush taxi pulls up, the forge-branch has burned away to embers.

You pay a second fare and ask the taximan to get your bag down from the top of the bus.

"But it's finished, Miss," the driver of the first bush protests. "We're in the process of fixing it."

"'Finished,' and 'in the process,' are not the same thing," you say. The men laugh.

As your bag hits the ground you see the driver of the disabled bus motioning for the passengers to come. You watch the passengers gather near the broken down vehicle as you sling your bag under your newly purchased seat.

The moon is up and full. Bats wheel in crazy circles above your head and the desert spreads its own calloused wings under the cold bluish light. You settle back and sigh when you hear the engine start.

Turning your head to look out the window, you see the driver of the first taxi swing up into his seat while four men, including Mr. Chaplin, take their places behind the bus. As the second taxi pulls off and passes the first, your mental camera frames and records the scene. Silent, dark and empty, the bush taxi is rolling down the road, pushed by four of its would-be passengers. The men grind the toes of their thin rubber sandals into the road and lean, hard, into the task of moving the vehicle meant to carry them. The old men, women, and children, shadowed and quiet as spirits, trail wearily behind.

The Black Impala

Katherine Melvin

That big old shiny black Impala of my brother Jack's stuck out on the side of the street like a craggy old wart sticks out on the side of a finger. It sat there waiting for him to come home from Southeast Asia where he was spending his summer courtesy of Uncle Sam. It was the simmering summer of 1967 when both the war and the country were heating up.

Everyone on the street, all seventeen homes, could see it. There was no missing a large black car parked in front of the only pink house sitting just as pretty as a picture in a green yard with a forest of trees for a frame. It was supposed to be seen. My father, retired Master Sergeant of this SOB peoples' SOB Army, never did anything without a point and he was the one who parked it there. It sat right in front of our house where the knuckle bent in the finger of the road.

The families who lived in the houses going up the hill saw it when they turned down the street to pull into their driveways. Everyone else lived past us and they had to go by it twice, coming and going.

That car sat in front of our house as a black metal memorial to my brother, only he wasn't dead. Yet. By joining the Army and going to Vietnam to fight for his country, PFC Jack Keselitus followed in my father's footsteps doing what my father did in World

War II and Korea. He was serving his country. Sarge was damn proud of it, too. Only my brother, he didn't volunteer like my father did. Uncle Sam came knocking on the door in the form of a US Postal service worker holding an official United States draft notice in his hand. It might as well have been a one way ticket to Vietnam.

On lazy do nothing days, my best friend Jamie Marie and me climbed on top of the Impala shrine to sunbathe. The curve of the windshield fit our backs just right. We wore tank tops and shorts to soak in the sun being absorbed into that shiny black hood. From our perch we kept an eye out for whoever might choose to drive down our street. It was the summer before we started high school and we could see no point to expending any energy other than to tan ourselves.

With our eyes set at barely open slits, we watched for our neighbors, the Dillard boys. That's if they dared to ride by. We didn't go out of our way to find them. Somehow, someway, they always managed to find us.

This particular afternoon was different, though, from the rest. I wasn't sitting on the car watching for the boys as much as I was trying to get closer to Jack. It was my way of touching him.

"What's the matter Angel?" Jamie Marie asked as she maneuvered her butt onto the hood and scooched back to the windshield.

I was already on the car leaning my back on the glass. My eyes closed.

"What are you thinking about?"

It was an innocent question.

"The news."

"Ah," she said. "We saw last night. My parents wondered if that's where Jack was."

"Yep. That's where we think he is."

"He's okay."

"How do you know?"

"I just do Ange. Inside here." Jamie Marie touched her stomach.

"You don't know anything!" I can't tell you why I lashed out at my best friend. She made me so mad I wanted to scream so I did. "The fighting and the bombing! That's right where he is! Do you hear what I'm saying? The Viet Cong bombed my big brother yesterday!"

A tear. I felt a tear on my cheek. Crap. I rubbed it away as fast as I could.

"I'm sorry Angel." She put a hand on my shoulder.

"What do you know? Your brother is safe." I dipped my shoulder so her hand fell off. Her brother ended up serving Uncle Sam stateside in Washington DC. "Jack could've been burned up by that flaming gas they drop on the jungles." My hands accented my words. I never could keep them still. "He might've been killed, Jamie Marie!"

There was nothing to say to that so we remained silent.

My parents and I learned on the CBS Evening News the night before that the Viet Cong bombed the area where my brother was fighting. Or at least where we thought he was. There had been no letters since the one telling us he was going into battle. Walter said that most all of the area was destroyed by Napalm, some kind of flaming fire gas, which we, we being the United States military, used to rid the area of our enemies. Walter Cronkite told us so and we believed him.

We watched the color footage of boys flown out by chopper. Some were alive. Others, it was easy to see, were not. We stared at the dirty, soot darkened soldiers who walked around in a daze in the background behind the reporter. TV made it feel like a movie, but I knew better. It was real. We searched for Jack's face. We hoped he was one of those battle weary soldiers.

I unclenched my fists. "I'm sorry."

Jamie Marie shrugged me off. "Me too," she said.

Jack was like a brother to her having known her since we were little kids. Just like hers was one to me. They teased and tickled and distressed us equally, no favorites.

"Look." Jamie Marie nudged me. She nodded her head toward my house. "Hey, Mr. Keselitus," she waved.

"Hello girls."

My father stood on the porch. He gazed up the street with a look like the prodigal's father must have had when he scanned the horizon searching for the return of his son. The wondering was too much for my father even with being a crusty old Master Sergeant and all. After a few minutes, he went back inside but not before he raised the largest American flag money could buy on the flagpole attached to our house. It hung limp in the heavy humid heat as if fluttering took too much effort for a flag whose colors were stained with so much blood.

We didn't bother with making up stories or quoting poetry. Jamie Marie and me, we were on guard duty. Looking. Waiting.

There was no telling when the military car carrying the Marines in dress uniform bearing the telegram would drive down our street. Or if they would. There was no telling anything that hot summer afternoon.

Mr. Dillard worked in his yard. He knelt on the hot asphalt driveway trimming the edge of the lawn. Every few minute or so, he wiped the sweat off his face with a handkerchief. Then he waded it up and shoved it into his back pocket. I wondered where the Dillard boys were. They weren't bothering us and they weren't helping him.

"Where do you think the boys are?" I didn't have to state which boys. "They usually have to help."

"Don't know," Jamie Marie said. "Don't care."

"Me either."

Time crawled.

"Boy it's hot," I said with all the strength I could muster.

"Yep."

Neighbors stood at their front doors. They glanced at our house and then up the street. They shook their heads then went back inside. They watched the news every night too so they knew what was happening.

It was late afternoon moving toward evening when we saw the mail car.

"Pretty late for the mail," Jaimie Marie pointed out. "He's normally here before lunch."

We watched the truck make its way from mailbox to mailbox depositing bills and letters and advertising.

"Maybe his schedule got turned around or something."

At my house, the driver stopped.

My father came to the door and stepped outside. He waited.

The mailman shrugged and waved to say there were no letters from the jungle as if it was his own personal fault. He handed me the flyers and some bills. I brought them to my father. We nodded "what can you do" at each other. We both hoped for more.

"Let me go tell your mother."

This time I sat on the hood and dangled my feet over the side of the car. I thumped them against the tire. Donny and Danny finally appeared and rode by a couple of times, but we didn't pay them any mind. We didn't have the energy to ask where they'd been. All effort focused on my brother and the wondering. The wondering if he'd be coming home in a box or injured or maybe even that he was fine and would return to tease us once more.

Jamie Marie sat up. Her hands shaded her eyes. "Look there," she said pointing up the street.

I turned to look. It was a long, long way to the top of the hill. I squinted and stared just to be sure, but I couldn't ignore the black sedan. It was a plain looking car.

I jumped off the Impala to get my father. Somehow he already knew. He and my mother were out the door before my feet hit the pavement. Everyone seemed to sense the car's presence. Neighbors stood in their front yards watching. It drove like the first car in a funeral procession only it was the only one.

My heart beat inside my chest like it wanted to push right through my ribs to the outside.

Before long the neighbors moseyed over to our yard forming a small clump by the side of the road. They stood by my parents watching. My Master Sergeant father of this man's Army put an arm around my mother and pulled her close.

That car, it didn't fly down the street and come to a stop at our feet. It moved in slow motion like some kind of film clip stuck at the wrong speed. Those soldiers were looking for the right house. We could see them staring at the numbers stuck in fake brass to the fronts of each home. Before it reached the black shrine of a vehicle sitting in the crook of the road, the sedan stopped. But not where we expected. It halted right in front of the Lieutenant's house, two doors up from ours, four down from the top.

The clump of people moved closer together as if the very unity of those beating hearts could stop what was about to happen. We watched the two Marines get out. They put on their hats, straightened their dress uniforms, and proceeded to the door in good fashion.

I didn't want the Lieutenant's wife to answer the knock. Don't! Don't do it!

She opened the door.

The Marines went inside with her, but they were back out pretty quick. I mean how long does it take to read a telegram telling you that your husband, your only husband and father of your children, served his country well by dying in the jungles of Vietnam?

It was a fact he settled his wife and family here on Mohegan Avenue because he knew they'd be cared for on a military street.

The services, they look after their own. He was right. Mrs. Lieutenant was invited to all the parties. The men checked in on her to see if there was anything that could be done around the yard or house. The women hovered. Jamie Marie and I pitched in with babysitting.

The clump of neighbors broke up. My parents went inside. Others went on home and a few walked over to the Lieutenant's house. They knew they'd be needed. The military really does know how to console its own.

And me, well, me and Jamie Marie climbed right back up on the Impala. Touching that car kept my brother alive. At least for one more day.

Cesar at the Laundromat

Gary M. Almeter

I had been teaching at private high school in Boston. My fiancée had been working at an academic press in Boston. What better way to test our mutual mettle than plying our collective skill sets in the Big Apple? I am neither too proud nor too immune to say that we thought that if we could make it there we could make it anywhere, both professionally and domestically.

The years I taught at a private high school in Boston, I taught a myriad poems and short stories by white American authors to boys who would go to some Ivy League school whether I was there or not. I wanted to teach at an authentic New York City public school, like in the movies. I wanted teaching to be a transformative endeavor - resulting in metamorphoses.

So that summer, the summer of 1998 when the world feasted on Bill and Monica and people left their jobs in droves for dot coms and wealth seemed possible just by walking out your front door, I delved into the works of black and Latino authors and prepared lessons therefrom. I was elated when I read Henry Louis Gates's essay "In The Kitchen" about the hair straightening rituals he endured as a child and used it as the foundation of an entire unit I called "Assimilation." I couldn't wait to empower and lead and transform.

The first day of school was enlightening. The kids I taught were poor but resilient, newly emigrated and proud. It became evident very early that they regularly endured more than any kid should. But they stayed kids. The students' reading levels made it apparent that they weren't ready for Henry Louis Gates. Nonetheless, I reveled in being a teacher. It seemed easy to make a difference. I called students in the morning to make sure they were awake and going to school and they respected me for that. I patted them on the back when they walked into the classroom. They were rarely touched with any affection.

Surprisingly, at least to me, my students were more responsive when they could escape into a new world rather than examine their own. My seniors had never read "Catcher in the Rye" so I taught that and they loved it, far more than they had "I Know Why the Caged Bird Sings." Stories of childhood trauma bored them they said with the aura of anyone who has been there, done that. Stories of people frolicking in other lands intrigued them. My freshman loved "Romeo & Juliet" far more than they had "The House on Mango Street." Oddly, they related to kids fighting with their parents much more than they could Esperanza's dreams of escaping her impoverished neighborhood. It turns out that empowerment came as readily and authentically from conquering the canon as much as it can come from stories of survival written by your people.

Quite a different phenomenon happened with the kids' writing. They were eager to look inward and share intimate details about their lives. When I asked kids to write fictional narratives I expected fancy sports cars and limousines, international trips and intrigue, but most of the time I got stories about gang bangers, abortion clinics, drug-addicted relatives and abusive uncles.

So they were simultaneously yearning to tell their stories while eager to hear the stories of someone else. I could understand that. I was eager to hear more about their worlds, about which I had little insight. I was also learning to see the value in expanding their world, fostering navigability through the white canon, even if it meant sacrificing awareness of their own. My goal had always been to provide them with the feeling that they had a place in public discourse; that they could be effective in whatever profession they chose; and to erase some of the cynicism that made them feel they could not make a difference. I was discovering a different pathway to that goal.

In December, I was tasked with going to listen to a band that my fiancée and I were considering hiring to play at our wedding reception. The Groove Bus was playing a holiday gig at the Windows on the World restaurant atop the World Trade Center's north tower. December is a particularly rough month in NYC, especially for those who do not live in a department store window or a neighborhood resembling such. The kids I taught were in what I would come to know as their chronic December funk, common with urban youth, precipitated by the onslaught of Christmas images and ideals and commercials. I found it exhausting – physically and emotionally. That summer, I had read "Santa Claus is A White Man" by John Henrik Clarke, the story of a black boy who encounters a racist Santa on his way to buy Christmas presents. I was determined, despite my recent epiphany, to read it with my classes and had done so that day. With disappointing results. So I secretly welcomed the opportunity to head out by myself and wallow.

I took the subway to the WTC, got off on the 105th Floor of the North Tower to several raucous holiday parties. I found Groove Bus and sat down at the bar. The Groove Bus played reception standards to which I listened disinterestedly, more intent on getting wasted than assessing their adeptness at replicating Kool and the Gang. I put my credit card on the bar and sat back to listen and watch the night's malfeasance unfold. It was a spectacular display; on several fronts. Outside, New York was lit up like a Christmas tree. Inside, there were hedge fund managers in sleek suits and with sleek hair frolicking with submissive women in festive crushed velvet dresses and trying-too-hard-to-be-festive stockings. I thought it all too spectacularly cliché to be true: the office party, the secretaries, the acquiescence, the yearning, the commuter train, the lip stick on the collar, the scents, the fornicating, the New Yorkness of it all. I, in my green sweater, blue jeans and brown loafers, seemed to be the only one not in a monochromatic shirt and tie and black suit. I was a confident man; but was learning that separateness can have a debilitating effect. I detected it with the haphazard and apathetic way the bartender made my drinks for me, the way girls seemed not to give me a second glance.

With regard to the economic disparity of the sort perpetually playing itself out in New York, I fancied myself both an observer and a participant. My students were poor. They wrote about things that astounded me. They had both a strength and a defeatism that perplexed me. I walked home from school feeling like the luckiest guy in the world; but after the walk home in one of the wealthiest zip codes in America, felt utterly despondent. So being here, amidst the excess, made me feel both disloyal and triumphant. At the very least, it was disorienting. For which world was I better suited?

Like a kid reading Shakespeare, there was an allure in the escape of the sort afforded by the WTC. In seeing how other people lived. In imagining their homes, their cars, their vacations, the shape of their swimming pools. Where nouns like summer double as verbs. But it also made me want to stand up and assert, "I am here too. Acknowledge me." Much like my kids did when they walked into a Gap and received no service.

After too much gin, I traced my steps back to the subway to wait for the 4-5-6. The next thing I recall I was being woken up by a conductor simultaneously shaking me and kicking me off the train with a mix of disgust, burliness and anger. My pants were wet; I had peed myself. I stumbled off the train. The cold and the wind sobered me up. I had clearly never been here before. I walked downstairs and saw from the sign on a produce that I was on West 167th Street. I had no Metro card and no money and decided that walking east was my best chance at finding an ATM.

It was late and there were no people. Anywhere. I walked past a few steel gated stores without seeing anyone, bumped into a few older men hanging out outside a bar another block east and saw a single older woman across the street. This is what it feels to be vulnerable I thought. This is how it feels to be scared.

After a couple more blocks, the urine on my jeans beginning to freeze, I heard someone say, "Mr. G" with both authority and confusion. It was Cesar, one of my students.

He was holding the door of a Laundromat open, gesturing me to come inside. His face evinced a look of sheer bewilderment. I followed him into the Laundromat and asked, probably slurred, "what are you doing here Cesar?"

"I live here."

"No, in the laundromat. It's almost 2:00 in the morning." Looking at my watch.

"I had to wash my mom's uniform. She didn't get home until about midnight and has to go to her other job in the morning and then right to her job after that so needed a clean uniform."

"A better question is what are you doing up here, Mr. G?"

I replied with nothing but an empty, shame-filled stare. And a few tears. I even felt my lip quiver from cold and disgrace as Cesar looked at my wet jeans and got a sense of what was happening.

"Laundry's almost done. We can go back to my house and my uncle will drive you home."

We sat in silence, me hoping I didn't but knowing I did smell and he nonchalantly finishing his math homework as though this sort of encounter happened all the time. The dryer buzzed a few minutes later. Cesar removed the light blue shirt dress and folded it expertly. It had "Broadway Commercial Cleaning" embroidered on the left chest, over a big sprawling cursive "B."

I walked with Cesar a few blocks back to his apartment, a six story brown brick building on 169th street, me in my piss-soaked jeans and sweater and barn jacket; Cesar in his jeans and white t-shirt and too-big black puffy coat. I waited in the vestibule as Cesar ran upstairs. The floor was littered with old mail, cigarette butts, dust balls. A few minutes later, Cesar and his uncle, a small man about my age, wearing Timberlands and a leather coat over a bath robe, came outside. The uncle, extending his hand, introduced himself, "I'm Javier."

"Gary," I said and shook Javier's hand, doing my best to convey some sort of authority, acting as though it wasn't nearly 2:00 a.m. and acting as though I wasn't his nephew's English teacher standing there with piss-soaked dungarees.

Javier looked at me with a friendly face that displayed no judgment. We walked about a block and stopped at a brown Monte Carlo, probably a late 1970s model, with a tiny Puerto Rican flag hanging from the rear view mirror. Cesar told me to get in front as he climbed in the back seat. We drove south; and rode in silence. New York was still lit up like a Christmas tree, and the towers were visible in the distance. Presumably Groove Bus was packing up their instruments. I, again as though the normal tenets of etiquette applied to the situation, asked what Javier did for a living.

"I am taking some classes at City College. In the meantime, just working for my uncle doing asbestos abatement."

"What kind of classes?"

"Working towards my degree in criminal justice. Hope to be a police officer and then work my way through law school."

It struck me that Javier was trying to impress me; me, the man who was sitting in piss-soaked dungarees in the passenger side of his car; the man who probably owed them his life; the man who seemed to know absolutely nothing about anything. The inherent absurdity and absurd unfairness of this struck me with some force – even then; even in that compromised state.

We crossed over one of the bridges onto the Harlem River drive. Javier asked where I lived and I mumbled "East 86th." I told Javier that the corner of York and 88th just off the FDR was fine but Javier said he'd be happy to take me home. For the first time, Cesar spoke, "Let him take you home Mr. G."

I opened the large squeaky car door at the front of my building, turned around and shook Javier's and Cesar's hands, only later realizing that I had not washed my own since pissing myself. I thanked them and held the seat forward as Cesar climbed into the passenger seat. He put down a magazine over the wet spot I had left.

I took the elevator upstairs, took off my jeans, washed myself, put on my pajamas, and then went to the hallway, threw my jeans down the trash chute and then stealthily climbed into bed.

I was ready for work and out the door before my fiancée woke up. I walked the three blocks to school, checked my mailbox, made some photocopies (kids would be doing worksheets that day as I was hung over as fuck) then went to my classroom where I waited for the tumult of the day – and my demise - to begin.

Cesar nodded hello when he walked into class. No smile, no snicker, no indication that anything was amiss and certainly no indication that anyone else knew what had happened a few hours before. Because no one else did know what happened. Or ever would know what happened.

And I didn't say anything to Cesar.

Until the following week, on the last day of school before Christmas break. Cesar stayed after class to help me clean up. We chatted about school stuff. He told me he wasn't looking forward to break because he was always alone. I stopped myself before I could thank him or provide any commentary on his neighborhood or strategies or coping mechanisms. And I just let him talk.

Asperger Syndrome:
An Affliction or a Gift?

Andrew McDowell

DIAGNOSIS

Autism is like a spectrum. My mother and I always envisioned it as such. Rather than all colors from red to violet, there exist several mental disorders classified as Autism Spectrum Disorders, ASDs. They are also known as Pervasive Development Disorders, PDDs. These syndromes share some common characteristics. Those who have them are characterized primarily by a deficiency in social and communicational skills, in addition to certain repetitive behaviors. However the behavior, and the severity of the condition for each patient, varies. Hence my mom and I saw a spectrum. One of the mildest of these disorders is known as Asperger syndrome. I have Asperger syndrome.

What exactly causes Asperger's remains undetermined. One theory is that it might be hereditary, since the disorder tends to run in families. But in my case, nobody in my family has been diagnosed. Asperger syndrome seems to affect between .024 to .036 percent of children, although the exact number is unknown. According to the Asperger's Association of New England, estimates of Asperger's in the world population range between .36 to .71 percent. It is also apparently more common in boys than in girls. The

AANE gives a ratio of 4 to 1. Why boys seem to suffer from it more so than girls is another unsolved mystery. I am not alone in having such a disorder, but then again it is unique for each patient, so I am alone.

Asperger syndrome was first described in the 1940s by Austrian pediatrician Hans Asperger, but would not become an official diagnosis, a unique disorder in its own right, until several decades later. Most children with Asperger's are diagnosed between ages of two and six. I was not. I was originally thought to have Tourette syndrome, which I was diagnosed with at the age of four. Tourette's is a neurological disorder, noted for visible compulsive ticks. It is certainly not an Autism Spectrum Disorder. It would not be until 2005 when I was officially recognized as having Asperger syndrome, *not* Tourette syndrome. By then, I had already entered high school. I was fifteen.

How I actually got diagnosed is an interesting story. By the time my parents and I came back to the United States from living in Japan, they suspected there was something more about me that was different. It was through a chance reading of a library book about Asperger syndrome that my mom recognized similarities between my behavior and what she read, saying as much to my dad. A colleague of dad suggested I get tested at Kennedy Krieger, which according to my mom is the country's foremost authority on children with ASDs. First, we met a Dr. Rubenstein, and he proposed I go for the full testing. It took some time before I actually went in to get an evaluation of my abilities and where I was on the spectrum.

It is difficult for children with Asperger's to empathize with other people and I still have difficulty empathizing. That is one characteristic of Asperger syndrome. But perhaps the most identifiable characteristic is an impairment of social and communicational skills. Interacting with other people for children with this disorder is extremely difficult. Even for me, even now in my early twenties as when I was little, it is hard for me to engage in conversation, or to make any friends. When I was little, I was pretty much the quiet type, a loner with few true friends. Even at college I had trouble engaging in conversation when sitting with friends in class or the dining hall. Children with Asperger's also usually feel uncomfortable in social situations. As a toddler, whenever out with my parents I usually acted shy, hiding behind one of them.

Understanding language in context, making eye-contact with other people, understanding and interpreting facial expressions and body language, these are all other symptoms seen in children with Asperger's. That does explain why I did poorer in critical reading than in math or writing on the SAT. My parents bought me a book specifically for kids with this disorder. It contains common phrases, slangs and their meanings, like a dictionary. I look at it all the time, but I am still learning what things mean. Making eye-contact is definitely a problem for me too. Many times whenever my parents talk with me or after I talk to someone I am reminded about trying to make eye-contact. Doing interviews or acting onstage has helped me get better at it.

It is difficult for me, to use my mom's words, to quiet my mind, which results in trouble sleeping all the way through the night. Roughly 73 percent of children with Asperger's experience sleeping problems. These problems do not so easily go away as they do in kids without Asperger's. I usually I have trouble falling and staying asleep. There are times when I wake up in the middle of the night. Often if there is something on my mind, stressing me out, I find that is when I just cannot sleep soundly.

While unafraid to tell people I have Asperger's, there are some details I will not go into deeply, because I consider them too embarrassing. Children with Asperger's may display some unusual or repetitive behavior or movement. I suppose however, some are not too embarrassing that I can discuss them. I pace a lot; my mom is constantly asking me to stop. I just do it whenever I get bored. Dad keeps reminding me of when I am doing a "Did you know" scenario as he calls them, explaining things to people. For him that is annoying. I gradually came to understand and respect that, but even now there are times when it is hard to resist telling people facts I think most do not know, and I can forget having told specific facts to specific people in fact. It is almost like a habit with me.

Asperger children might even have certain rituals or preoccupations that they feel bound to follow. Alternating those rituals is simply impossible. Sometimes I like to organize things in certain ways. As a boy, I collected metal trains from the *Thomas the Tank Engine* series, organized them on the coffee table more than playing with them. Some photographs survive showing me doing that. As far as routine goes, I certainly have always liked an order to things. My mom says as much too. I never like a disruption to a routine. I always feel most uneasy when settling into a new routine. But once I in, I settle down.

Interests among people also vary like a spectrum. For children with Asperger's, that range can, and usually is, limited to a small number. But for me, identifying those was actually troubling to the point where I had to ask my mother what she thought they were. Her answer was only that at certain times I concentrate on certain topics, I learn about them, remembering everything I learn. She said that once after school to a teacher of mine in middle school, although I do not recall which one. When with my parents talking to Dr. Rubenstein, it was mentioned I usually bought books listing facts. I read those kinds of books a lot (I had one that I had I had taken in the car at the time, a Christmas present, with facts on space, Earth, animals, and the human body; I corrected dad on how to pronounce narwhal; it was used as an example).

Interests vary, sometimes depending on the place or the situation. When I lived in Japan at age nine, Pokemon was the big thing in school. I did my best to learn about Pokemon. Now at the age of twenty-one, I think one of the interests that has really gripped me is creative writing. I think the nice thing about this interest is that I can utilize other interests and write tales. I might even write a story, a play even, about someone with Asperger's who tries to cope with it and adjust his life. I think it would make great drama. My interest in genre fiction in particular is interesting, considering most adults with Asperger's prefer nonfiction over fiction, a fact that is reported by the Adult Asperger Test.

Asperger syndrome might be seen as a disability, but children with it can show exceptional talents in various different fields. Like interests, for these children those talents are usually small in number. Once again it was difficult for me to figure out what these talents are, and my mom once again thought it was my great memory. I can remember a lot when it is a topic that I like. Or, perhaps I have yet to discover exceptional talent in something if I even have it. I would like to think that it is a talent, even if I still receive critiques from friends and family. I have trouble with certain things in writing such as character depth, though in terms of plot and details I have no trouble. Well no one is perfect at anything, but we strive to do our best in spite of our flaws.

People with Asperger syndrome in spite of their lack in communication skills, often show intelligence that is usually average or higher, so they can function very efficiently. Certainly for being intelligent, I am thankful. Getting good grades and complements from others on what I do does boost my spirits. Getting good grades in school has made me feel happy always. Unlike other ASDs, linguistic development (learning language through hearing and repeating) and cognitive development (learning perceptional skills and information processing) are largely maintained, even if they are limited. In a way I am lucky, gifted, even if I am afflicted with this disorder.

The fact that I can function at a high level than most other autistic people comes to mind every time I think of the autism spectrum. Former neighbors of mine had a daughter who had severe autism. Out of respect I will not reveal their names. But she could not speak. She had to go to a special school. She shall be a dependent for the rest of her life. Having seen her, I know that I am lucky. Were my condition not so mild, I could never have gone to school, write stories, and not even just go out in public. So even though I have an affliction, I am still lucky, and gifted.

TREATMENT

There is no medicine for Asperger syndrome. It can never be prevented, nor can it be cured. A person like me who has an ASD has it forever. In effect it is a part of me. It will continue affecting my outlook and my life. But that does not mean Asperger syndrome cannot be treated. It is possible to seek help in the form of interventions. Unfortunately, as the AANE clarifies, there is no single intervention for every autistic person due to it varies amongst them all. Several websites talk about treatment and intervention. But for my part, thinking about it, well, sometimes I just do not want to think about it at all.

At the time I was diagnosed, it initially meant very little to me. But it was certainly eye-opening for my parents, particularly my mom. She bought books about Asperger's, some written in fact by people who had it, discussing how it affected their lives and outlooks. The neuropsychological report also recommended a number of websites for my mom on the disorder. So far I have not read any of them. In my defense, perhaps it had something to with routine. Or more likely I just never really had an interest in reading them. To others, not reading them may seem ignorant of me. I can understand why. Certainly when I was younger, I gave very little thought toward my disorder.

The assessment of the Kennedy Krieger Institute's neuropsychological evaluation from when I was fifteen said my active skills were equivalent to a child aged eight and nine months. It noted also I largely talked about my own interests and had little sense of the evaluator's. Learning all these facts by reading their assessment after all those years, I do feel bad. Mom and dad also have pointed out how at times when I say things I misuse words and say things that are insulting to others but were never intended to be. Again, that makes me feel guilty. Guilt and sadness like anger I have trouble letting go of. Once they overtake me, they do not go away easily. Then again, it is what I am (but I do wish to take a stronger interest in other peoples' interests). People say we should be proud to be who we are. Every person is flawed, something that literature and writing taught me. That is not a bad thing, but that does not mean one should try to just live with their flaws. Otherwise I would not have tried to moderate them.

Being diagnosed late I had grown up not knowing about it, not knowing I was different. Those around me knew I was different though, and because of my behavior I was a target for bullying. I had difficulty, according to the Kennedy Krieger evaluation, trusting other people due to those years of being bullied. Though I hate having been bullied, the experience taught me to hate all teasing, to empathize with those who are bullied, and to value loyalty, and honesty. I am grateful knowing I am at heart a good person. Certainly by the time I graduated from high school, it had been a while since I was last bullied, so something must have changed in me.

Sometime after being diagnosed, I do not remember how long afterwards, but I went in for sessions at Kennedy Krieger late in the afternoon. These sessions were for anger management. As a target for bullies, it was extremely difficult for me to let go of anger, or control it. But anyway, a series of little videos from those sessions stick out in my mind. They starred little children, certainly none in adolescence, displaying three reactions to bullying: cold (crying, giving in), hot (unleashing anger), and cool (ignoring, joking, explain feelings calmly, etc. so as to not get sad or mad). It never was easy containing anger, but I tried, I did my best to be cool in those situations. I can certainly remember times when I got really angry before I even knew I had Asperger syndrome. The aftermath of unleashing anger is never pleasant, always painful. I learned my lesson.

At the time of the assessment, I participated in very few extracurricular activities. A few which I did get involved in were the golf team and drama club. It was recommended that I continue on with them and join several other clubs, in order to make new friends. The drama club especially helped me come out of my shell. I got to work with several people, and do something which I really enjoyed. I was only in the golf team freshman year, and by senior year I had joined many more clubs than just drama, tried a few but did not stay, and had several friends. I was chosen as "Most Likely to Succeed." I was part of both the Homecoming and Prom Court (I sort of campaigned for those two, but not the superlative). But for neither I had a date. I still have not had a girlfriend. My timidity is something I still have to work getting over.

I specifically went to St. Mary's College of Maryland because it was a small environment with a small body of students, like all the other colleges I applied to. Having Asperger's and not being comfortable in large crowds then small classrooms, I do not believe I would have done well in a large university. Doctor Rubenstein in fact recommended St. Mary's College, a college to which he donated a boat. I joined several other clubs at college, and made many more close friends. Nowadays, telling people that I have Asperger syndrome is nothing I try to avoid. While I deliberately do not tell everyone, I do not hide the fact that I have it. I have improved at one-on-one conversations to the point that where I happen to mention my condition, some are surprised, claiming they never would have guessed. My parents too are proud of how far I have come.

In my junior year of high school, there was a walk to help raise awareness of autism. A teacher had an autistic young son whom she introduced us to. He later led us in reciting the national anthem. Eventually, given that I had an ASD, I chose to speak out about my condition to everyone the day of the walk. Some friends afterwards said I did a good job, but I felt I stuttered and hesitated all the way through it. I stated that I would be walking for those less fortunate, those with severer autism. Once again I was reminded I am one of the lucky ones. I hope to support autistic research more in the future.

Asperger syndrome is indeed a part of me. Maybe I do still have certain behaviors that I wish to hide for fear of embarrassment. Maybe I do still do things not empathetic to others, or stay out of crowd and conversation. But the fact that I have Asperger syndrome I never attempt to hide, not from anyone. It does come with its deficits, but also its surpluses, like everything in life. I may be a loner at times, but I am also an intelligent, honest, hard-working, conscientious person with a family that loves me dearly. I cannot imagine what kind of person I would have been, if I did not have Asperger syndrome. It is nothing for me to be ashamed of, not anymore.

Last Dance in Havana

Cherie Magnus

Am I dreaming or on the moon? Havana at night is surreal. I'm not prepared for the darkness, the decay lit only by florescent lights casting an eerie gray glow over the crumbling arcades and torn up sidewalks. There is no neon, no advertising save for a few dim *Viva la Revolucion!* billboards, no commercial signs, few streetlights, only the occasional low watt gray porch light. Havana is the darkest city I've ever been in. The ghostly figures I see moving among the shadowy ruins might be waltzing to Prokovief in Disney's Haunted Mansion.

But going about their business in the dark are the colorful, vibrant, infinitely practical Cuban people moving to the Cuban rhythms heard everywhere in the streets and in their daily lives. If Fidel is the father of modern Cuba, music is the mother of its people.

Being in Havana now feels like I've journeyed back through the decades to not only another place, but another time, an island Brigadoon, an eroded Atlantis found. This is the land of pirates and buccaneers, of Conquistadors and Castro, of castles and kings and an exotic museum of Communism. A tropical paradise that some thought to be the Garden of Eden, with a bloody history that includes American presidents, the Mafia, and the search for the Fountain of Youth. And all of this is in a five-hundred-year-old country only ninety miles from the U.S.!

I didn't realize any of this before my arrival—all I knew about Cuba growing up in California was Castro, Communism, and cigars. But I wasn't in Havana to get involved in history or politics. I came here for the timeless pleasures of music and dance. I knew when I saw "The Buena Vista Social Club" that I had to go to Cuba. The old American cars cruising under the spray from the waves crashing against the Malecon to the song "Chan Chan" — that scene made me cry, and travel all this way to explore why I was affected so much by a piece of popular music.

The U.S. Government only allows Americans to travel to Cuba and spend dollars if they have relatives there, if they are journalists, or for educational and cultural exchanges. Otherwise we are violating the *Trading With The Enemy Act.*

The basis for my trip is a cultural exchange—I'm with a group licensed to teach the Cubans Argentine tango and they will teach us to dance salsa. Rather ironic for a native Californian of mixed European ancestry to presume to teach Latinos a Latin dance. But for Cubans, Argentine tango is as foreign as West-Coast Swing.

Our group of overseas tango dancers stay at the Hotel Seville in Habana Vieja, the heart of the tourist center. Built in 1908 and now owned jointly by Cuba and France and recently restored, its large public spaces and guest rooms are plain but comfortable and the Roof Garden on the ninth floor is absolutely stunning with old world grandeur.

Like other world capitals, Havana, too, is its architecture. But the general disintegration of its once-grand Spanish Colonial mansions, now with flags of colorful laundry on the rusted baroque balconies, only adds interest to the history-starved Norte Americano's vacation, plus the benefit of lots of photo ops. We can go to Europe if we want to see the golden arches nestled among ancient edifices.

I see how Havana satisfies our nostalgia for days gone by, for what we've lost. Here we are young forever, here we can see the world that perhaps our parents inhabited. And so very much better than a trip to Main Street U.S.A. at Disney World. Havana is real, a romantic, mysterious, two-faced and forbidden time warp. We visitors murmur to each other, looking at pastel palaces turned into tenements, imagine what it was like *before!*

Our group of American, Canadian, Argentinean and Cuban dancers meet daily either in the hotel or at the Union Arabe across the street on the Prado, where giant loudspeakers constantly blast salsa, the blanket term for son, mambo, Afro-Cuban, chachacha, rumba and other forms of Cuban music. At first the dance exchange is a struggle for everyone; the visitors can't move their hips sufficiently in the salsa classes, and the Cubans can't not move their hips as the tango requires.

After classes we all go together to dance clubs in a big bus. This is one country where women can feel more free and have more fun when going in a group. Especially if you are a dancer. In Buenos Aires I boldly go alone each night to the tango halls where I dance until dawn with no problems. There is a strict formal code of behavior there, and in all my trips to Argentina, I never once had any sort of difficulty.

Cuba doesn't work like that. There are very few salsa clubs per se, and I wouldn't recommend a foreign woman entering them alone, hoping to dance, as she might in Buenos Aires. The Cubans dance all the time, but informally at parties and casual gatherings. Most can't afford the clubs priced in dollars, so there are typically only other tourists, along with the prostitutes who follow the foreigners around like birds on buffaloes.

At the Casa de Musica in Miramar, the music takes several in our group back to the hotel in a taxi due to the decibel level of the live band. But for the rest of us, drinking Cuba Libres and mojitos, we reach an altered state of consciousness on the packed dance floor with body heat, hypnotic drums, repetitive hip movements, and pheromones filling the smoky air. Eduardo tells me it's like the *camels*, the public buses, or *guaguas*, which cram hundreds of people into their hump-backed spaces—never too full to take more passengers, and always a sensual experience: heat, smells, and lots of body contact.

Another night we went to Salon Rosado at El Tropicale, an open-air club on three levels. Supposedly for the over-40 crowd, it's just as sex-charged as the Casa de Musica. I look around and enjoy the sight of black and white faces mixing happily in impromptu conga lines and a *rueda de casino*, a kind of circular salsa Virginia Reel. Everyone dances with everyone else regardless of age, color, language, national origin, politics, or marital status, and everyone exults the power of the music with their bodies.

Suddenly the electricity goes out and we are thrown into a silent darkness lit only by the full moon behind the silhouettes of towering trees. The stars blaze in the black bowl above us. Accustomed to the rolling blackouts that are an every day fact of Havana life, people calmly light cigarettes and socialize. When the power returns twenty minutes later heralded by blasts from the band's brass section, the dancing renews its frenzy.

When dancing in Havana it doesn't matter what kind of shoes you wear, or if you wear any at all, or how you're dressed (the Cubanas favor Lycra), or placing your feet with precision. You just let the music take you! People dance alone, in twos, threes, and even in large circles. Details don't matter, just move! The music insists.

Liza, the island's only tango teacher, along with my new Cuban "sister" Miriam, her college student son Fernando, and I become a foursome who dance tango wherever we can persuade the ubiquitous live musicians to play one. The organizer of the group told us when we arrived that if we go someplace with a Cuban, we must pay, as prices are in dollars and they don't have any. It is worth it to me to treat my Cuban friends; I am exhilarated by Havana, the music, and the Cubanos. I can't get over the fact that this vibrant musical and friendly culture has been close by all my life and I knew almost nothing about it. I feel like I never want to leave. *The love I have for you I cannot deny.*

When not dancing, I'm a typical tourist. I'm agog at the medieval architecture, the Spanish tiles, the colonial blue of the restored woodwork, the surprising lack of propaganda. Every day I eat *morros y cristianos* (black beans with white rice.) And oh yes, I walk along the Malecon kissed by Caribbean salt spray, hearing "Chan Chan" in my head. Whenever I get tired, I hop on a bicitaxi and am cycled back to the Seville, usually for a dollar.

There is virtually no shopping in Havana. In La Moderna Poesia, a large modern bookstore on Calle Obispo, I take a photo of the empty shelves, so strange for one used to a crammed Barnes & Noble. The elegant old pharmacies have polished mahogany shelves bare but for herbal remedies. The department stores feature sanitary napkins in the window as if they were straight from Paris.

Che Guevara's image is everywhere—Che in Cuba is like Christ in Rome. And the paternal words and visage of *El Maximo* hover over the city, faded but ubiquitous.

Cuba goes far out of its way to make tourists happy, as tourism is now their biggest industry. But the tourist doesn't get a good look at the other Cuba, the one of the Cubans.

The Cubans live in two worlds: their own and that of foreign visitors. Cubans get two government TV channels; tourists get CNN and satellite stations in several languages. There is the peso market and the dollar market (and the meeting of the two in the black market.) There are Cuban taxis, restaurants, hotels, markets, and shops, where only pesos are spent. Then there are the dollar stores, products and services.

The Cubans may not have a lot of material things, but still they know how to enjoy themselves. Luckily the best things in life are free, because the Cuban people glory in their music, their dance, and their sexuality. They smile, their dispositions are sunny, and they are the most full of life folk I've ever met. I am enchanted.

Havana feels very safe. There are police everywhere, in front of every important building, on every street corner, looking into every bar and restaurant for illegal activity. Cadres of security people are stationed throughout all the tourist hotels, making the tourists feel safe, but also keeping the Cuban people out. It is against the law for a Cuban to be in a tourist hotel room—"for their own protection." One of our Cuban dancers makes a mistake; after class she teaches a dance step to two American women in their room and the chambermaid reports her to hotel security. Rudely ordered downstairs and to show her identity papers, the plea of the two Americans doesn't prevent her breaking down into tears. She is mortified—and so are the Americans.

We tourists see the old-fashioned charm and warmth that is carefully orchestrated for us to see. We love Cuba, but we also can leave. A new Cuban friend Rey, a bellboy at the hotel, says that since the triumph of the Revolution, no one dies of hunger as before. Samuel Johnson wrote that freedom is "the choice of working or starving." The next day Rey tells me how his brother's raft sank on its way to Miami...

There is a huge shantytown of illegal "aliens" across the bay and behind the enormous statue of Jesus Christ. Starting out some years ago as a collection of fifteen shacks, now there are more than five hundred paper, plastic, and scrap wood hovels in the area known as Casa Blanca. There is no water, electricity or latrines, but at least the police leave them alone due to the close-knit group of squatters, normally afraid of the police once they leave Casa Blanca. These thousands of people are mostly from the east of the island, and are called Orientals. They are illegal because there is no freedom of movement in Cuba; you must stay where you are assigned. But as bad as life is for them in Havana, it must be so much worse at the island's other end for them to leave home and families to come west and not to be able to have a legal job, their ration books, or a place to live. They survive by hustling—buying fruit in the country and selling in Havana, odd jobs, playing in musical groups, avoiding the ubiquitous police as much as possible because they don't have the proper I.D. papers. If caught, they are fined, if the fines are not paid, they can go to prison for over 3,000 days and work their fines, off in hard labor for the state.

I got to know one of these people, a man from Guantanamo, who couldn't legally work with our dance group but sat in the band with his friends. During one free afternoon, he took me to Casa Blanca to show me around. A musician, writer, and a poet, a gentle, sensitive, sweet soul, I prayed he would stay healthy and get enough to eat until the time comes when he could take a legal job. He and the other residents of Casa Blanca dance, laugh, play dominoes, swim at the beach, smoke and drink rum, and make music (on improvised instruments if they have to) whenever and wherever they can. Casa Blanca is the other face of Cuba and the *Triumph of the Revolution.*

Although being American I feel guilty about so many things, the Cuban people don't seem to blame us. "It's not you, it's your government officials," is the gracious way they put it. They seem to realize (but not vocalize) the fact that the glory of the Revolution is past, and since the end of the Soviet Union, they are simply waiting. And making the best of it. They wait for better times, and meanwhile are determined to live.

Cubans are amazingly resourceful, innovative, and clever at creating what they want and need out of what they have. The classic American cars that they keep running on cannibalized parts, clunky Soviet engines, and spit, are the most famous example of Cuban ingenuity. But there are many, many others that you see when you visit. Making silk purses out of sows' ears is a national talent.

At our farewell party in the Roof Garden of the Hotel Seville, there's an all-girl salsa band, and performers in thongs and feathers. We all dance salsa, and many of us dance tango. We exchange promises to write, but without easy access to the Internet in Cuba, email is difficult, and regular mail is extremely slow, unreliable, and censored. The Cubans ask when we will return, and wistfully grow silent when the time comes for them to say when they might visit us.

I have bonded with Miriam and young Fernando. She is about my own age, bilingual, and a journalist for the radio, which means that unlike most Cubans, she has access to email. We vow to keep in touch, and I swear to myself that I will be back soon somehow. This exotic land and its people have grabbed my heart.

Now handsome Esequiel grabs my hand, saying, "Vamos, mami!" and we dance our last dance. I have learned this week that his sad expression is probably more due to his need for dental work than his mood.

I awkwardly give drummer Carlos a tube of heavy-duty cream for his rough hands, as lotion—like soap and shampoo—is almost impossible to come by due to the U.S. embargo. I promise to send Eduardo a Spanish/French dictionary. I give Teresa, Yolanda, and many other women satin baseball hats I'd brought with me. And to Rey, I give the most treasured gift of all, a bottle of aspirin for his mother. Here in Cuba, when locals whisper to you in the streets, it's indeed about drugs, but it's Tylenol, cough syrup and antacids they are interested in.

I receive a small blackface doll in a rumba costume, a necklace of watermelon seeds and shells, a postcard of Havana—precious mementos I cherish. The Cubans and the visitors laugh together without end the last night, all of us with happy Cuban faces. If we didn't laugh, maybe we'd cry.

Rey whispers to me with a smile, "I see you are sad because you are leaving. Look at me, I cannot leave, yet I am happy."

As the old Soviet-era propjet takes off for Nassau the next morning, I see the ribbons of highways bisecting fields of sugar cane down below, empty but for only the occasional vehicle. Before long the turquoise sea sparkles in the sunlight. The United States and its many choices is so far away. I hear "Chan Chan" in my head, and I'm crying.

Oysters

Matt Hohner

"At night—the soft shuck of everything on earth
softly sliding away into space."
—Mary-Alice Daniel

Every now and then you emerge from the soil,
exhumed out of the darkness by a backhoe
on a street in Baltimore. There you are. A body part,
serial-killed by history. An ear who last alive heard
the water-muffled splash of steam-driven paddle wheels.

A layer of flat calcium flakes under the asphalt
and macadam, under bricks and cobblestones.
Strata of progress. Archaeology of amnesia.

On a February rainy night in Annapolis you beckon
from ice in market stalls and raw bars barnacled in your
old-man skin, haired by algae, moist protein bodies inside,
dressed ugly, but the locals' lusty gazes shuck you with their eyes.

Bullets punched outboards and chests
over you. Men died for your flesh.

A beach on the Wicomico down from Salisbury where
the old packing plant once stood: kayakers tread your bones
to get to the tannin'd currents racing past. Women's hands
eighty-years dead last held you, dispatched your silent,
blind, bivalve lives inside with a poke-slip of their knives.

John Smith said he could walk across your shoals at low tide.
You have run aground many a foolish captain who lost track of you.
Once your legion filtered the whole bay in days; now
it takes you a year. There's mercury in the mud. There's lead.
How do you taste without that metallic after-singe?

Give me that cool glide at the back of my throat.
Give me your pornographic flavor.

I'll eat you until my blood runs silver.

what the cicada said to the brown boy

Clinton Smith

i've seen what they make of you
how they render you a multiplicity
of mistakes
they have undone me as well
pulled back my shell and feasted
on my flesh
claimed it was for their survival
and they wonder why I only show my face
every seventeen years
but you
you're lucky if they let you live that long
i could teach you some things, you know
have been playing this game since before
you knew what breath was
this here is prehistoric
why you think we fly?
why you think we roll in packs?
you think these swarms are for the fun of it?

i would tell you that you don't roll deep enough
but every time you swarm they shoot
get you some wings, son
get you some wings

The Last Hours of Summer

Matt Hohner

North Central Railroad Trail, Gunpowder River, Maryland

Already the air has chilled. In the last hours of summer,
September light lingers crisp on wood barnsides bleaching
under the dry blue dome. What bends to hold us, what filters
through us, what remains of us as the winds shift? What of us
recedes in the pewter horizon haze? A lone crow punctuates
the meadow below the old railway bridge. Snapping turtle
big as a hubcap lolls downstream with the current over
gravel bed shallows. Acorns knock through oak branches
down to the soft loam. Slow crickets trill in the cold shade.

In a field by the far road the first rows of fat, ripe corn falls
between giant mechanized pincers, then stillness in the corduroy
of stubble left behind. The empty ache. Brisk sigh lifts the canopy
along the river's edge. The crow, languid fragment of smoke,
lifts from the meadow, dissolves like thought into the afternoon.

Winners of the
Maryland Writers' Association
2015 Contest

Gary M. Almeter lives on one of the coziest streets in Baltimore with his wife, three children and Beastie, their beagle. He is an attorney in Towson, an Orioles fan, a bibliophile, a cinephile, occasional runner, former New Yorker, former Bostonian and perpetual Buffalonian. His work has appeared in *McSweeney's* and *The Good Men Project*. (*1st prize, creative nonfiction*)

Matt Hohner holds an M.F.A. in Writing and Poetics from Naropa University in Boulder, Colorado, where he won the 1996 Ted Berrigan Scholarship and the 1996-97 Honors Scholarship. His work has appeared in numerous publications, most recently in *Free State Review*. Hohner lives in Baltimore. (*1st and 3rd prizes, poetry*)

Cherie Magnus, a California native, was a dance research librarian in the Los Angeles Central Library and a dance critic for local newspapers. Many of her articles on dance, books, travel and international culture have been published in magazines, professional journals, and several anthologies. She is the author of two memoirs: the award-winning *The Church of Tango*, and *Arabesque: Dancing on the Edge in Los Angeles*. (*3rd prize, creative nonfiction.*)

An aspiring writer, *Andrew McDowell* lives with his family in Gambrills. He studied History and English at St. Mary's College of Maryland. His main interests are poetry and novels. (*2nd prize, creative nonfiction*)

Debra McGhee was a Peace Corps teacher in Niger, West Africa. She is now works for a civil rights agency within the federal government. She is a winner of the Anthony Ura Award for fiction award by Pennsylvania State University, and has published non-fiction pieces in *The Georgetowner, The Alexandria Gazette*, and several other publications. She lives in Crownsville with her husband and son. (*2nd prize, fiction*)

Katherine Melvin is a writer living in the Gaithersburg, MD area. Her non-fiction works have been published in *Catholic Digest, Today's Christian Woman, Christianity Today*. She has just completed a Master Novel II class at the Bethesda Writers' Center. (*3rd prize, fiction*)

Barbara Mujica is a novelist, short story writer, and professor of Spanish literature at Georgetown University. Her novels include *Frida*, which appeared in seventeen languages, *Sister Teresa*, and *I Am Venus*. She is the mother of a Marine and faculty adviser of the Georgetown University Student Veterans Association. *Jason's Cap* is based on a true story. (*1st prize, fiction*)

Clint Smith is a teacher, poet, and Ph.D. candidate in Education at Harvard University. His work has been published by *GRAVTAS, Write Bloody* and others. (*2nd prize, poetry*)

Maryland Writers Association Acknowledgments

Primary Judges

Holly Morse-Ellington has published essays and photographs with *Wanderlust and Lipstick, Matador Network, Three Quarter Review, Baltimore Fishbowl, Outside In Literary & Travel Magazine, Urbanite, The Journal of Homeland Security, The Washington Times*, and elsewhere. She is an editor for *Baltimore Review* and the publicist for award-winning singer-songwriter, Victoria Vox. Holly is also the State Vice President of the Maryland Writers' Association. Holly and Jason Tinney co-authored the play, *Fifty Miles Away*, winner of the Frostburg State University Center for Creative Writing One-Act Play Festival 2015. They write and perform music as Limestone Connection.

Born in India, **Lalita Noronha** is a research scientist, science teacher, poet, author, and a fiction editor for *The Baltimore Review*. Her literary work has appeared in numerous journals and anthologies such as *Crab Orchard Review, The Cortland Review, The Baltimore Sun, The Christian Science Monitor, Get Well Wishes (Harper Collins)* among others, in the US, India, Canada and Australia. She is the author of a short story collection, *Where Monsoons Cry (BlackWords Press)* which won the Maryland Literary Arts Award and a poetry chapbook, *Her Skin Phyllo-thin (Finishing Line Press)*. Other credits include a Maryland Individual Artist Award in fiction and awards from *Arlington Literary Journal*, Dorothy Daniels National League of American Pen Women, Maryland Writers' Association (fiction, creative nonfiction and poetry) and two Pushcart nominations in poetry and creative nonfiction. She has also been featured a few times on National Public Radio, WYPR, *The Signal*, and currently serves as the State President of the Maryland Writers' Association.

Secondary Judges:

Dominique Cahn was born in Port-au-Prince, Haiti and moved to New York City when she was six years old. Raised on New *York* City's Upper Westside, she uses fiction to explore issues of immigrant identity. She received her Bachelor of Arts from Princeton University and a Masters in Public Health from Yale University. She has 15 years of work experience in international health and in government relations and health care policy. She has travelled extensively in the former Soviet Union and lived in Kazakhstan for two years. She serves as reader for the *Little Patuxent Review*. She currently resides in Bethesda, Maryland with her husband and two daughters.

Brandi Dawn Henderson is a traveling writer, on regular journeys that prove truths to be no strangers to fictions. She co-created and edited *Outside In Literary & Travel Magazine*, a resource dedicated to promoting cross-cultural understanding through global storytelling. She wrote a relatively successful expat column and an utter failure of an advice column for a year in New Delhi, is the editor of the travel anthologies *Whereabouts: Stepping Out of Place* (2Leaf Press) and *(T)here: Writings on Returnings* (Martlet & Mare Books), and has had work published in a variety of journals. She now resides near Portland with a red-bearded outdoorsman and two dogs, Lola and Cormac McArfy. www.outsideinmagazine.com

Shenan Prestwich is a writer, poet, editor, and Washington, DC native recently transplanted to Portland, OR. Publishing in a wide variety of venues both in print and online, Shenan holds a Master of Arts degree in writing (with a concentration in poetry) from Johns Hopkins University and her first full-length collection of poetry, *In the Wake*, was recently released from White Violet Press. She has served in an editorial capacity for publications such as *Magic Lantern Review*, *Outside In Literary and Travel Magazine*, and *Prompt & Circumstance*. You can follow her at http://shenanprestwich.com.

Emily Rich is the non-fiction editor of *Little Patuxent Review*. She writes mainly memoir and essay. Her work has been published in a number of small presses including *Little Patuxent Review*, *Welter*, *River Poet's Journal*, *Delmarva Review*, *the Pinch* and *r.kv.r.y*. Her story "On the Road to Human Rights Day" was a notable entrant in the 2014 edition of *The Best American Essays*.

Lynn Stansbury is a fiction writer, community medicine physician, and medical writer and editor. She served in the Peace Corps in Guatemala in the Vietnam War era, finished a BA in art history in 1970, helped start community clinics in California, then went on to public health and medical training in Hawaii. She has worked in the gyppo logging communities of Montana, in American Samoa, among the Oglala Sioux of North Dakota, for the Colorado Black Lung Program, and, back in California again, in clinics for Spanish-speaking farm workers. After the Army transferred their family to the DC area in 1993, she spent eleven years at the NIH before joining the research group at Maryland Shock Trauma. She finished the Hopkins MA in Fiction Writing in 2010, and is working on another novel as her thesis work for her MFA in Creative Writing at the University of Washington, Seattle.

Pat Valdata is a Cecil County writer with an MFA in writing from Goddard College. Her poetry publications include the book *Inherent Vice*, published by Pecan Grove Press in 2011, and a chapbook *Looking for Bivalve*, which was a Pecan Grove Press contest finalist in 2002. Pat has twice received Individual Artist Awards from the Maryland State Arts Council for her poetry. In 2013 she was awarded a grant from the Mid Atlantic Arts Foundation for a residency at the Virginia Center for the Creative Arts. Thanks to this grant and residency, she completed the manuscript for a forthcoming book of poetry that was awarded the 2015 Donald Justice Prize. Pat has taught writing and literature for the University of Maryland University College (UMUC) since 2007.

Final Judges:

Ned Balbo's third book, *The Trials of Edgar Poe and Other Poems* (Story Line Press, 2010), received the 2012 Poets' Prize, and the 2010 Donald Justice Prize. *Lives of the Sleepers* (University of Notre Dame Press, 2005) received the Ernest Sandeen Poetry Prize and a ForeWord Book of the Year Gold Medal. *Galileo's Banquet* (Washington Writers' Publishing House, 1998) shared the Towson University Prize for Literature. He has received the Robert Frost Foundation Poetry Award and the John Guyon Literary Nonfiction Prize, and he is co-winner of the 2013 Willis Barnstone Translation Prize. His poetry, prose, and translations are out or forthcoming in *Able Muse, Beltway Quarterly, Cimarron Review, Gargoyle, Hopkins Review, Iowa Review, River Styx*, and more. He lives in Baltimore with his wife, poet-essayist Jane Satterfield.

Susan Muaddi Darraj graduated from Rutgers University with a Master's degree in English Literature. She is currently Associate Professor of English at Harford Community College. Susan is the author if *The Inheritance of Exile*. Her new book, *A Curious Land*, won the 2014 AWP Grace Paley Award for fiction and will be published in 2015.She is currently an editor for *Barrelhouse Magazine*, and along with Dave Housley and Julie Wakeman-Linn, she co-founded the annual Conversations & Connections Conference in Washington DC. Her stories, essays, and reviews have appeared in numerous anthologies and journals, such as *Mizna, New York Stories, Banipal, Calyx, Little Patuxent Review, Solstice,* and elsewhere.

Apprentice House is the country's only campus-based, student-staffed book publishing company. Directed by professors and industry professionals, it is a nonprofit activity of the Communication Department at Loyola University Maryland.

Using state-of-the-art technology and an experiential learning model of education, Apprentice House publishes books in untraditional ways. This dual responsibility as publishers and educators creates an unprecedented collaborative environment among faculty and students, while teaching tomorrow's editors, designers, and marketers.

Outside of class, progress on book projects is carried forth by the AH Book Publishing Club, a co-curricular campus organization supported by Loyola University Maryland's Office of Student Activities.

Eclectic and provocative, Apprentice House titles intend to entertain as well as spark dialogue on a variety of topics. Financial contributions to sustain the press's work are welcomed. Contributions are tax deductible to the fullest extent allowed by the IRS.

To learn more about Apprentice House books or to obtain submission guidelines, please visit www.apprenticehouse.com.

Apprentice House
Communication Department
Loyola University Maryland
4501 N. Charles Street
Baltimore, MD 21210
Ph: 410-617-5265 • Fax: 410-617-2198
info@apprenticehouse.com • www.apprenticehouse.com

www.ingramcontent.com/pod-product-compliance
Lightning Source LLC
Chambersburg PA
CBHW020919180626
46816CB00007BA/2473